The subject mat[ter] and vocabulary have [been] with expert assistance, and the brief and simple text is printed in large, clear type.

Children's questions are anticipated and facts presented in a logical sequence. Where possible, the books show what happened in the past and what is relevant today.

Special artwork has been commissioned to set a standard rarely seen in books for this age level and at this price.

Full-colour illustrations are on all 48 pages to give maximum impact and provide the extra enrichment that is the aim of all Ladybird Leaders.

A Ladybird Leader
man in the air

Written by James Webster
Illustrated by Gerald Witcomb

Publishers: Ladybird Books Ltd . Loughborough
© Ladybird Books Ltd 1973
Printed in England

Men have always wanted to fly

An old Greek story tells of Icarus.
He made wings of feathers and wax.
The sun melted the wax and
he fell into the sea.

Men watched the birds flying

Men tried to make wings of their own.
Early birdmen were very brave.
They could not fly like birds.
Often they hurt themselves.

Hot air rises

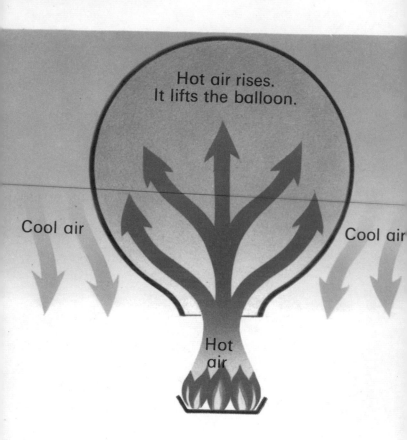

Hot air rises.
It lifts the balloon.

Cool air

Cool air

Hot
air

Men found that hot air rises.
They made a fire balloon.

The first flight

The Montgolfier balloon

Nearly two hundred years ago,
two brothers, named Montgolfier,
flew in this hot air balloon.

Hydrogen gas also rises

Blanchard and Jeffries' balloon

Some balloons were filled with a gas called hydrogen.

A balloon filled with hydrogen crossed the English Channel.

Giffard's airship

Balloons could not be steered.

Henry Giffard made a
steam-driven airship.

This could be steered.

The first aircraft to fly with an engine and propeller

In 1903, the brothers Wilbur and Orville Wright flew this aircraft in America.

They flew for 12 seconds.

Bleriot flew from France to England in 37 minutes.

This was the first aircraft to fly across the English Channel.

Men fight in the air

In the First World War, men fought
in the air for the first time.

About fifty years ago, Alcock and
Brown flew this aircraft
from America to Ireland.

They flew at about 118 miles (190 km) an hour.

Today, aircraft cross the Atlantic at more than 600 miles (966 km) an hour.

17

An air-raid in the Second World War

In the Second World War, the aircraft
were bigger and faster.

They carried many bombs
and destroyed cities.

Early jet aircraft

In the Second World War, the first jet engines were used.

With these engines, aircraft could fly much faster.

See what happens !

Blow up a balloon

Pinch its neck

Let go and see what happens

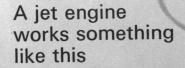

A jet engine
works something
like this

21

Carrying people by air

More and more people want to travel
by air.
Bigger and bigger aircraft are made.

This Jumbo Jet can carry 400 people.

Carrying goods by air

Most goods are carried by ship to other countries.

Here is a cargo ship.

An aircraft carries goods
faster than a ship.

It costs more to send goods by air.

Carrying cars by air

Some people take their cars abroad.
Aircraft like this can carry them.

Carrying mail by air

Letters can be sent much more quickly
by air mail.
They can reach any city in the world
in a few days.

Holidays by air

In cold, wintry weather, people may fly to another country.

In a few hours they can be sitting in the hot sun.

Sometimes aircraft are used to sow very large fields with seed.

Fields can also be sprayed from the air to kill pests and weeds.

Aircraft help to save lives

An injured man goes to hospital.

In some countries, nurses and doctors
fly long distances to people
who are ill.

Sport in the air

Gliders do not have engines.
Glider pilots use air currents to fly
for hours at a time.

Parachutes

Some people drop by parachute
for sport.
Soldiers also can drop by parachute.

Helicopters

A helicopter can stay still in the air.
It can save lives because of this.

A helicopter can land troops
almost anywhere.
It does not need a runway.

The aircraft cockpit

Here is the cockpit of a large, modern aircraft.

There are many things in it that the pilot must watch.

The aircraft crew

The people who fly the aircraft
and look after the passengers
are called the crew.

A new type of aircraft

This aircraft can go straight up and straight down like a helicopter.

It can fly faster than a helicopter.

A very fast passenger aircraft

A passenger plane has been made
which can fly at 1,350 miles
(2 173 km) an hour.

A modern airport

1 Radar scanner
2 Control tower
3 Passenger terminal
4 Fuel depot
5 Aircraft hangars
6 Fire Station
7 Multi-storey car park
8 Car parks

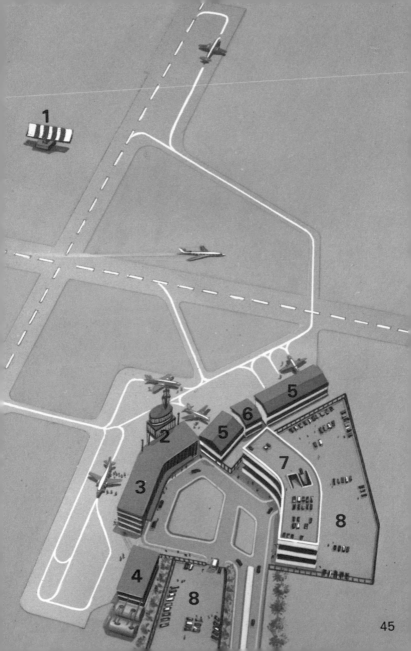

45

A rocket aircraft

This rocket aircraft has flown at more than 4,500 miles (7 242 km) an hour.

The shape of aircraft to come?

One day, aircraft like this may fly
in space.
They will have rocket engines.

Aircraft can cause problems

The noise from aircraft can spoil people's home life.

It can also damage buildings.

The gases from aircraft engines
can spoil clean air.
Airports need a lot of land.

'Mono' means 'one'.
A monoplane has
one wing.

'Bi' means 'two'.
A biplane has two
wings.

'Tri' means 'three'.
A triplane had
three wings.

A flying boat can land on water.

A ski plane can land on snow.

A helicopter can land on a building with a flat roof.

Some distances by air

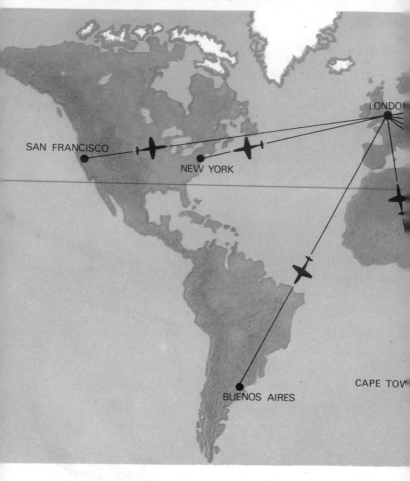

London to New York	3,441 miles	(5 538 km)
San Francisco to London	5,354 miles	(8 616 km)
London to Buenos Aires	6,919 miles	(11 135 km)
Cape Town to London	6,010 miles	(9 672 km)